BRANCH LINE BYWAYS

VOLUME TWO

Central Wales

G. F. Bannister

FRONT COVER: Springtime on the Mid-Wales Railway in April 1954. BR 2MT 2-6-0 46506 heads south near Llanidloes with a local passenger train from Moat Lane Junction to Brecon. *Photo: T. B. Owen/Colour Rail*

BACK COVER, TOP: Nantmawr branch cameo. BR 2MT 2-6-0 46510 leaves White Gates Crossing north of Llanddu and heads up towards the quarry in April 1965. *Photo: G. F. Bannister*

BACK COVER, BOTTOM: GWR 0-6-0PT 5774 stands in Blaenau Ffestiniog Central in August 1955 with an afternoon passenger train to Bala. *Photo: John B. Snell/Colour Rail*

TITLE PAGE:
Porthywaen in its heyday, 18 September 1936. GWR 0-6-0T 819 hurries away from the station with the Llangynog local bound for Oswestry whilst 0-6-0ST 680 awaits clearance of the single line section to Llynclys Junction with a train from the Steetley Lime and Basic Company's sidings. The narrow gauge Crickheath Tramway makes a neat diagonal between the two standard gauge lines. *Photo: the late Selwyn H. P. Higgins courtesy National Railway Museum*

First published 1987

Designed by Nigel Trevena
Typeset by Delta Graphics, Falmouth, Cornwall
Halftone photo reproduction by Oxford Litho Plates Ltd, Botley, Oxford
Printed by Century Litho, Penryn, Cornwall
Bound by Booth Bookbinders, Penryn, Cornwall

ISBN 0 906899 26 5

**Published by
ATLANTIC TRANSPORT PUBLISHERS
Waterside House Falmouth Road
Penryn Cornwall TR10 8BE
England**

Dedication

To all the railwaymen in Mid-Wales both past and present, for without their help, co-operation and enthusiasm many of the pictures would never have been recorded.

Foreword

So comprehensive is the literature of the British railway scene today that it becomes progressively difficult to add anything more, in fact many of the lines contained herein are already the subject of definitive works. The titles listed below were of immense help in preparing photographic captions for the present volume and to their authors and publishers I offer my thanks and hope to let the pictures tell the rest of the story. I have deliberately avoided the thorny problem of spelling Welsh place names by adopting the official Great Western Railway version at the risk of upsetting the purists — as George Behrend remarked in his wonderfully nostalgic book 'Gone With Regret', the "Great Western was careless with English names and indifferent to Welsh ones", witness CEMMES ROAD, PLAS-Y-COURT and WOMBOURN.

The Author

Geoff Bannister, BA (Hons) is a lifelong railway enthusiast, photographer and author of three other books on the railways in Central Wales and the West Midlands. Until his retirement he ran the Geography Department at a Wolverhampton grammar school.

Note

All mileages quoted are those given in the Working Timetables and Supplementary Appendices of the Great Western Railway and British Railways (Western Region). The GWR Working Timetable facsimiles are those dated July 3rd-September 24th 1939. Maps are not to scale.

Photographs

Unless otherwise credited, all photographs in this book are the work of the author.

Bibliography

The following sources were consulted during the preparation of this volume and are recommended for further reading:-

GEORGE BEHREND: Gone with Regret; Jersey Artists
JAMES I. C. BOYD: Narrow Gauge Railways in Mid-Wales (1850-1970); Oakwood Press
LEWIS COZENS: various guides to the Mawddwy, Kerry and Llanfyllin Railways; Aberayron Transport, all published privately between 1947 and 1957
ERIC TONKS: The Shropshire and Montgomeryshire Railway; Industrial Railway Society 1972
WILFRED R. WREN: The Tanat Valley Light Railway; Oakwood Press
RAILWAY CORRESPONDENCE & TRAVEL SOCIETY: Locomotives of the GWR Part 10; published by the RCTS
REX CHRISTIANSEN & R. W. MILLER: The Cambrian Railways, two volumes; David and Charles
REX CHRISTIANSEN: Forgotten Railways North and Mid-Wales; David and Charles
C. C. GREEN MBE: Cambrian Railways Album, two volumes; Ian Allan North Wales Branch Line Album; Ian Allan
WORKING TIMETABLES & SUPPLEMENTARY APPENDICES of the GWR and BR (Western Region)
Railway Magazine
Railway World
Trains Illustrated
Stephenson Locomotive Society Journals and 'Last Train Souvenir Brochures', various years 1955-62

Acknowledgements

For additional illustrations especial thanks go to Andrew Bannister, James I. C. Boyd, Roger S. Carpenter, R. C. Riley, T. J. Edgington (National Railway Museum) and John L. Smith (Lens of Sutton). I am indebted to Brian Timmins who again offered constructive criticism in the preparation of the manuscript, Ron White of Colour-Rail who provided unstinted co-operation in the search for colour illustrations, Pam Westwood for deciphering Welsh place-names on her typewriter and Jan Endean for making such excellent prints from my ageing negatives.

I am very conscious of the warm response to the first volume in the BRANCH LINE BYWAYS series and I would like to take this opportunity to thank the many readers who have been kind enough to write such complimentary letters. It is hoped that the present volume evokes a similar reception.

Tettenhall, April 1987

GWR 57XX Class 0-6-0PT 5774 with a specially strengthened Saturday train from Bala climbs steadily through the barren uplands between Teigl Halt and Manod with a Blaenau Festiniog train on 18 April 1959. *Photo: James I. C. Boyd*

Introduction

This second volume in the BRANCH LINE BYWAYS series covers a number of lines in the former counties of Montgomery, Merioneth and north Cardigan. Some were conceived as purely local concerns eager to connect with the outside world, mineral exploitation provided the stimulus for the construction of others, whilst a minority were promoted with the carriage of cheap coal, general merchandise and agricultural transits in mind. Income from passenger traffic was often of secondary consideration, a fact reflected in the relatively early passenger closures of 1931 on the Kerry, Corris and Llanfair Caereinion lines. Initial promotional optimism never seemed to flag in spite of financial difficulties but where goods traffic was once more substantial and more lucrative a number of branches survived for freight well into the 1950s.

Such obscure lines with their bucolic charm, antiquated motive power and erratic working methods provided the focus of my railway interest. Living within easy access to Mid-Wales proved a great advantage, and for good measure freight trains even ran on Saturdays.

The photographic challenge posed an entirely different set of problems in the early 1950s. Journeying to Abermule one never knew for certain whether a Dean Goods engine had been rostered for the 9.30 am Oswestry to Newtown Class K freight, or even whether it would take time out during the early afternoon to potter up the steeply graded grass-grown track to Kerry. Anticipation was a major part of the pleasure then as now — forehand knowledge would have eliminated the challenge.

When the railway ingredients for a photograph did gel, the fickle Welsh weather usually had the final say. Central Wales is not notable for record sunshine rates; in fact cloud cover, usually ten tenths, and constant drizzle appeared the norm rather than the exception or so it seemed in those far off days.

In 1948 well over a dozen GWR branches served communities in Central Wales, today the count can easily be accommodated on the fingers of one hand and these include the tourist orientated Vale of Rheidol and Welshpool and Llanfair narrow gauge railways, together with two truncated branches serving Blodwell Quarry and Trawsfynydd Nuclear Power Station. Sadly the remainder have all passed away, although a number of station buildings survive under private occupation.

In 1986 it is still possible to sample the flavour and immerse oneself in genuine byway atmosphere at Porthywaen or Maentwrog Road although the trains are few and far between, access to a weekly or even daily special traffic notice is now not only desirable but essential! *GFB*

Llynclys Jcn~ Llangynog

The Tanat Valley was yet another struggling concern where actual traffic volumes never matched expectations. It was worked by the Cambrian from the outset and was absorbed by that company in 1921, by which time the line was in the hands of a receiver.

There were ten stations on the branch (if one includes Porthywaen) in just under 16 miles, including three crossing places, Llanrhaiadr Mochnant, Llangedwyn and in an emergency, Blodwell Junction. The expected growth of mineral traffic never materialised, except at the eastern end of the branch in later years, and distances between stations varied from close to ridiculously distant — in the case of Llanrhaiadr Mochnant it was a mile and a half!

The TVR in its heyday typified the rural branch line of the border country. It had everything, splendid tranquillity, gated and non-gated crossings, mixed trains and it provided a haven for Ungrouped, lightweight, often time-expired tank engines eminently suited to working the lightly laid track and tight curves. Such antiques were culled from such far away counties as Cornwall and Berkshire. The line was also the last stamping ground, until 1947, of those fussy little Cambrian 2-4-0 tank engines and lightweight 0-6-0s, both the products of Messrs Sharp Stewart of Glasgow. Without exception they ended their days at Oswestry, and what a fascinating place that could be in the late nineteen forties.

RIGHT: GWR 0-4-2T 5812 awaits departure with an Oswestry train two years before premature closure was precipitated by the 1951 winter crisis in the domestic coal industry. Note the old Cambrian Railway's eight-wheel coach on the branch even at this late date. A stone wagon in the station yard represents the last vestige of the mineral traffic which sustained the line for over forty five years, originally lead and slate, giving way to granite for stone chippings. Three granite quarries developed in the vicinity of Llangynog but only one remained active at the end and most of its output formerly carried by rail had by then been usurped by road transport.
Photo: James I. C. Boyd

ORIGINS:	Porthywaen Mineral Branch (opened 1863) from Llynclys Junction-Porthywaen (Cambrian Railways), Tanat Valley Light Railway Company (opened 1904) from Porthywaen-Llangynog (Independent)
LENGTH:	15m 71ch
OPENED:	5 January 1904
CLOSED:	15 January 1951 (Passenger)
	1 July 1952 (Freight: Llangynog-Llanrhaiadr)
	5 December 1960 (Freight: Llanrhaiadr-Blodwell Junction)
RULING GRADIENT:	1 in 64

ABOVE, LEFT: The dwindling daily freight continued to run as far as Llangynog until the middle of 1952. The aftermath was to be six years of dereliction before the demolition gangs set about their work. As late as 2 May 1957 the station still retained its light railway atmosphere and Cambrian Railways semaphores as if it were not dead but sleeping.

ABOVE, RIGHT: Penybontfawr, the penultimate station on the TVLR, viewed eastwards on the same day from the road crossing after closure. The nameboard has disappeared but otherwise not much else has changed. The buildings are of standard pattern for the line, the station (waiting room, ticket office and toilets) and goods shed constructed in timber clothed in corrugated iron. A large yard on the left of the picture was used to store iron pipes and materials in connection with Liverpool Corporation's construction of a second aqueduct from Lake Vyrnwy in 1904.

RIGHT: Llanrhaiadr Mochnant, the most important intermediate station on the branch was also the most luxuriantly appointed by TVLR standards. It possessed a crossing loop, two platforms and all standard station appurtenances including a separate ladies WC tacked on to the booking office/waiting room on the up side. Llanrhaiadr became the railhead after 1 July 1952, when diminishing traffic in coal, lime fertilisers and animal feedstuffs provided the only source of income when the stone traffic finished. Ivatt 2 46509, in BR lined green livery, waits to leave for Oswestry with the meagre daily goods. By the time this picture was taken on 25

October 1954 the Ivatts had replaced all the Oswestry 'oddities' on branch line work. The Tanat Valley retained most of its Cambrian signals until the very end.

More traffic was on offer on 10th May 1956 as 46524, another of the batch of Ivatt 2s allocated to the Central Wales Division, picks up speed having negotiated the ungated crossing over the Llanfyllin road at Llangedwyn. By this date the former passing loop had become a repository for crippled wagons.

Llynclys Jcn — Llangynog

TANAT VALLEY and NANTMAWR BRANCHES.

Down Trains. **Week Days only.**

M.P. Mileage.	Miles from Oswes	Miles from Blodwell Junc. and M.P. Mileage.	STATIONS.	Ruling Gradient 1 in	Point-to-Point Times	Allow for Stop.	Allow for Start.	Empty Train. WO	Pilot.	Mixed WO	Mixed WX	Goods	Goods	Mixed MT FO	Pass. WTh SO	Goods RR SX	Mixed SX	Pass. SO	Pass. Runs first Wed. in each month V
					Mins.	Mins.	Mins.	a.m.	a.m.	a.m.	a.m.	a.m.	a.m.	a.m.	p.m.	p.m.	p.m.	p.m.	p.m.
M. C.	M. C.	M. C.					1	6† 0	6 50	7 25	8 5	8 30	10 5	11 20	2 15		4 25	5 25	8 45
	3 51		b OSWESTRY .... dep.	80 F.	13	1	1		7 33		8 13	8 45	10 20	11X28	2 23		4 33	5 33	8 53
			b c Llynclys Junction { arr. dep.					6 8	7 15			Y 8 55	10 42		2 27	3 0	4 37	5 37	8 57
1 40	4 55		Porthywaen .... ,,	63 R.					7 25	7 37	8 17	ST		11 32	2 34		4 44	5X44	9 4
2 40	6 11		c Blodwell Junction ... arr.	73 F.	11	1				7 44	8X24	—	10 55	11 39		3 13			
		M. C.									N								
		16	a Blodwell Junction ... dep.	73 R.		..	1	—					11 10	—		3 20			
			Llanddu { arr. dep.	52 R.	2	1	2	—					11 14	—		3 24			
		1 34	a Nantmawr .... arr.	42 R.	10	1		—					11 35	—		4 10			
													11 48			4 23			
3 17	6 68		c Blodwell Junction ... dep.	73 R.	2	1	1	6 18		7 45	8 25	CR		11 40	2 35		4 45	5 45	9 5
4 31	8 2		Llanyblodwell .... ,,	64 R.		1	1			7 49	8 29	CR		11 45	2 40		4 50	5 50	9 10
5 51	9 22		Glanyrafon .... ,,	64 R.	9	1	1			7 54	8 34			11 50	2 45		4 55	5 55	9 15
7 20	10 71		Llansilin Road .... ,,	130 R.	6	1	1	6 33		7 59	8 39	CR		11 55	2 50		5 0	6 0	9 20
			Llangedwyn { arr. dep.	66 R.		1	1			8 4	8 44	ST		12 0	2 55		5 5	6 5	9 25
9 11	12 62		Pentrefelin .... ,,							8 5	8 45	CR		12 1	2 56		5 6	6 6	9 26
10 42	14 13		c Llanrhaiadr { arr. dep.	88 R.	15	1		6 40		8 11	8 51	9X50		12 7	3 2		5 12	6 12	9 32
			Mochnant \ { dep.							8X18	8 57	10 20		12 13	3 8		5X18	6 18	9 38
11 51	15 22		Pedair Ffordd .... ,,	100 F.		1				8 23	9 3			12 14	3 9		5 20	6 20	9 40
13 28	16 79		Penybont Fawr .... ,,	89 R.	8	1	1			8 30	9 10	CR		12 19	3 14		5 25	6 25	9 45
15 71	19 42		c LLANGYNOG .... arr.		8	1		7† 5		8 42	9 22	11 0		12 26	3 21		5 32	6 32	9 52
													12 38	3 33		5 44	6 44	10 4

V—Will also run on Saturday, August 5th. **Y**—Will cross 7.45 a.m. ex Llangynog at Llynclys Junction on Wednesdays.

3 minutes allowed between Porthywaen and Blodwell Junction, and 3 minutes between Penybont Fawr and Llangynog for the opening and closing of road gates.

THE STEETLEY LIME AND BASIC COMPANY'S SIDINGS.

N—The engine will work from and to Porthywaen as required, with traffic to and from the above Sidings.

RIGHT: Ivatt 2 46524 approaching Llanyblodwell. Originally provided with Vignoles flat-bottomed rail, the Tanat Valley was relaid with chaired bull-head rail by the GWR by 1947. The freight was allowed ninety five minutes to cover the 10½ miles between Llanrhaiadr Mochnant and Llynclys. Tidy ballast, vegetation cut back and neat fencing gives a manicured appearance, how different from some other former GW byways featured in this book!

BELOW: Llansilin Road station viewed westwards from the road crossing in 1956. With the exception of the GW chaired track and the removal of the station waiting room this tranquil scene remains much as it was fifty years ago. Two wagons of coal are being unloaded at the end of the loop by the local merchant.

TOP: Blodwell Junction — originally Llanyblodwell ʊɪ the Potteries, Shrewsbury and North Wales Railway and not to be confused with the Tanat Valley station of the same name — exercised control over four different route directions during the early years of this century, two of which appear in this west facing view, taken from the Llanfyllin road overbridge (A491). In this September 1937 view, the Tanat Valley Light Railway veers to the right towards Llangynog at the end of the loop, while the stub of the original PS&NWR route to Llanymynech can just be identified in the distance. Behind the photographer the TVLR continued eastwards towards Porthywaen, diverging after two hundred yards from the PS&NWR which ran another mile and thirty four chains before terminating in Nantmawr quarry. *Photo: the late R. K. Cope*

MIDDLE: The forces of nature contracted the Tanat Valley railway even further on 5 December 1960, when the service had to be cut back to Blodwell Junction. Yet another Welsh branch line was forced out of business by a raging river, for the Tanat not only weakened a bridge west of Llansilin Road but also 're-aligned' the permanent way.

The corrugated iron 'Gents' still stands on the platform as Ivatt 2-6-0 46509 returns from Llanrhaiadr on 25 October 1954. Today, Blodwell Junction has been swept away and an earth mound marks the position of the platform but ballast trains coming to load at the Amey Roadstone Corporation's quarry still reach the other side of the Blodwell road bridge, where a new run-round loop has been constructed by British Rail.

BOTTOM: A Tanat Valley line passenger train between Porthywaen and Llynclys Junction on August Bank Holiday Saturday 1935. The locomotive is GWR 1196, one of a pair of ex-Cambrian small side tank 2-4-0s built by Sharp Stewart in 1866 and not finally withdrawn until 1948. *Photo: H. F. Wheeller*

Small GW tank engines from various absorbed companies which appeared in the Central Wales Division after the grouping, such as 680, 1308 and 1331, provide prime examples of the "heterogeneous collection of locomotives" mentioned in the text which wandered all over the Cambrian branches of mid-Wales until the late 1940s and early 1950s, all ending their days at Oswestry, 'haven for the lightweights'.

RIGHT: GW 0-6-0ST 1331 shunts the Lion Yard at Porthywaen in the summer of 1947. The one and a quarter mile long branch to Porthywaen from the Cambrian main line at Llynclys Junction was opened in 1863 and forty years later the majority of the line was incorporated into the Tanat Valley Light Railway. The quarries at Porthywaen provided a very valuable source of stone and agricultural lime. 1331 began life as Whitland and Cardigan Railway No.3, built by Fox Walker and Company in 1877.

BELOW: GW 0-6-0ST 1331 leaves Porthywaen with a trip goods bound for Llynclys Junction in the summer of 1949. Note the sheeted and hooded lime wagons. *Photo: the late Selwyn H. P. Higgins courtesy National Railway Museum*

Two very nostalgic views of Porthywaen in the mid-1930s with former Liskeard & Looe Railway 2-4-0T GWR 1308 *Lady Margaret* and Alexandra (Newport & South Wales) Docks and Railway 0-6-0ST GWR 680 easing trains of lime wagons out of the sidings.

TOP: The Tanat Valley line to Blodwell Junction, and Llangynog commenced its course on the left but more noteworthy, in the foreground, lies the 2ft 6in gauge track of the Crickheath Tramway. This 1½ mile long tramway connected Porthywaen to Crickheath Wharf on the Shropshire Union Canal and pre-dated the Porthywaen Branch of the Oswestry and Newton Railway from Llynclys by forty years, the latter opening on 1 May 1861 and crossing the Tanat Valley branch on the level. To the right of Porthywaen signal box, mixed gauge track with a common running rail on the up side carried both the Cambrian line and the Crickheath Tramway towards Whitehaven Pit. The tramway closed in 1913 but rails remained in-situ until 1939.
    Constructed by Andrew Barclay in 1902 *Lady Margaret*'s long association with the Tanat Valley line began after the grouping and with the exception of a brief spell at Exeter whilst working the Culm Valley Railway from Tiverton Junction to Hemyock in 1929 she remained at Oswestry shed until her withdrawal in May 1948. *Photo: courtesy J. L. Smith collection*

BOTTOM: GWR 680, a standard Peckett 0-6-0ST built in 1891, also ended her days at Oswestry in 1948. Your author can well remember a sighting of 680 dumped at the back of Stafford Road Shed, Wolverhampton awaiting attention in the factory sometime during January 1945. *Photo: the late Selwyn H. P. Higgins courtesy National Railway Museum*

Llynclys Jcn — Llangynog

ABOVE: Always kept in immaculate external condition, *Lady Margaret* is posed for an 'official' photograph at Porthywaen. The engine was re-built by the GWR at Swindon in May 1929 with a top feed boiler. *Photo: courtesy J. L. Smith collection*

BELOW: GWR 0-6-0 898 shunts the Nantmawr branch in the summer of 1935. She eventually became the doyen of the light Sharp Stewart 0-6-0 goods engines purchased by the Cambrian in 1878 (CR No.14 *Broneirion*). Originally constructed for the

Furness Railway in 1875, the engine was re-built by the Cambrian in 1897 and later received standard GWR boiler fittings. She was not withdrawn until 1947 as last of class and just failed to make the British Railways era. The mineral line from Blodwell Junction (formerly Llanyblodwell PS&NWR) opened in 1866, and became the north west extremity of the ill-fated Potteries, Shrewsbury and North Wales Railway. Although the 'Potts' main line closed in 1880, stone traffic on the Nantmawr section survived successively under the aegis of the Cambrian, the GWR and BR but heady aspirations of reaching the Welsh Coast at Porthdinlleyn foundered in the lime quarry at Nantmawr. At the time of writing the track remains in position from its junction with the extant portion of the Tanat Valley line at Blodwell Quarry, difficult to identify and permanently barred by a veritable forest of sturdy saplings sprouting unchecked between the boundary fences.

The longest remaining section of the 'Potts' now lies moribund and unlikely to rise again from the dead, waiting perhaps for Colonel Stephens' second coming. *Photo: John L. Smith collection*

RIGHT: Still performing the same duty on 3 September 1947, 898 soldiers on at Nantmawr, during her last year of active existence. *Photo: the late Selwyn H. P. Higgins courtesy National Railway Museum*

BELOW: The light railway atmosphere still prevailed on the Blodwell Quarry branch on 3 September 1986 at Porthywaen Crossing. Class 37 diesel locomotive 37241 is flagged across the A491 main road from Llynclys to Llansantffraid. The former station platform is still extant behind the hedge, although the site of the extensive rail complex of sidings and branch lines has long since disappeared under the surrounding boskage. *Photo: Andrew Bannister*

Llynclys Jcn — Llangynog

LEFT: A loaded stone train from Nantmawr quarry is dragged across the road at Porthywaen some thirty years earlier by GW open-cab 2021 class pannier tank 2054 on 4 February 1948. Built at Wolverhampton in 1898, 2054 was not withdrawn from Moat Lane Junction until 1951. *Photo: James I. C. Boyd*

BELOW: Class 25 diesel locomotive 25037 heads westward towards Llanddu from Porthywaen School Crossing with a train of empty ballast wagons from Bescot on 23 July 1986. This remaining section of the former Tanat Valley Light Railway is notable for the survival of cast iron rail chairs inscribed "GW&GC Joint Rly".

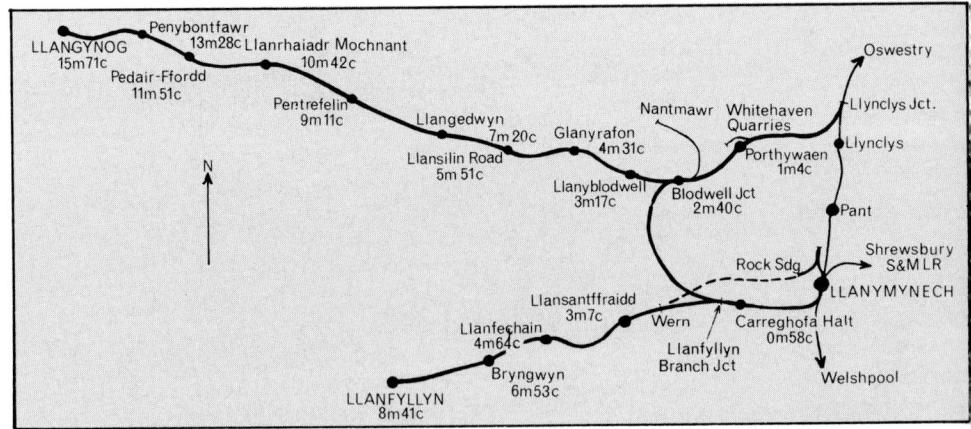

Llynclys Jcn — Llangynog

ABOVE: A pastoral scene in the Tanat Valley on 18 September 1936 encapsulates much of the Cambrian branch line charm of the Welsh Borderland. The Llangynog train bound for Oswestry ambles away from Llanyblodwell behind diminutive GW 0-6-0T 819, one of a trio of Lambourn Valley Railway tank engines which came into the Great Western fold, twice! The engine, built by Hunslet in 1903 for the LVR and named "Eadweade", was advertised for sale at Swindon and subsequently purchased by the Cambrian Railways in 1904, becoming their number 24.

At one time or another all three engines were put to work on the Tanat Valley and Kerry lines,

they also saw occasional service on the Van branch from Caersws. After the grouping 24 became GW 819 and continued her long association with the little

branches south of Oswestry until withdrawn in March 1946. *Photo: the late Selwyn H. P. Higgins, Courtesy National Railway Museum)*

Llanymynech~ Llanfyllin

ORIGINS:	Oswestry and Newtown Railway
LENGTH:	8m 41ch (from Llanymynech Junction South)
OPENED:	17 July 1863
CLOSED:	2 November 1964 (Freight) 18 January 1965 (Passenger)
RULING GRADIENT:	1 in 75 (1863-1896: 1 in 50)

The Llanfyllin Railway led a rather mundane, penurous and totally unexciting existence for most of its one hundred and two years. It did, however, lay claim to three notable distinctions. Firstly, it emerged as a fully fledged branch line of the Cambrian Railway, having been opened by the Oswestry and Newtown in 1863. Secondly, Llanfyllin became the busy railhead for the delivery of materials used in the construction of Liverpool Corporation's Vyrnwy Reservoir scheme from 1881 onwards, when vast quantities of cement and iron pipework for the construction of the dam and aqueduct were delivered over the Cambrian Railway system from Aberdovey Harbour on the Cardigan Bay coast. Last but by no means least, for thirty-three years the journey over the branch from Oswestry and Llanymynech performed a most unusual convolution which involved a double reversal at the latter place — all very confusing to the casual visitor. A new curve was opened in the 1896 rebuilding, allowing a direct approach to the branch from Llanymynech Junction South by way of the original Potteries, Shrewsbury and North Wales Junction Blodwell line, worked by the Cambrian since 1881, thence joining the original formation of the branch from Rock Siding at Wern by way of the new curve. In spite of the apparent innocuous course along the valley of the Afon Cain the 8½ mile line possessed some quite severe gradients.

The Llanfyllin Railway was typical of most Cambrian lines in that the volume of passenger trains far outweighed those of freight. Rex Christiansen and R. W. Miller aptly summed up the situation in their two volumes of Cambrian Railway's history when they wrote "few railways had covered so much ground to serve to few people and so few towns". This truism not only applied to the trunk routes but especially to the rural branch lines like Llanfyllin, which only served agricultural communities.

ABOVE: Non auto-fitted 0-4-2T 5816, introduced by the GWR for working light branch lines, brings a Llanfyllin bound train into Llanymynech on August Bank Holiday Saturday 1935. The coaches are Swindon built twin set W6776/6777W, two non-corridor brake compos brought into use on the branch in 1933. The picture reveals a tantalising glimpse of a Shropshire and Montgomeryshire special passenger excursion with an ex Midland Railway bogie coach in view. Regular passenger services in the S&MR ceased on 6 November 1933. *Photo: H. F. Wheeller*

LEFT: Fourteen years on and great changes have taken place. The S&MR platforms at Llanymynech are now under the control of the War Department who occupied the line in 1941. Lime wagons occupy the down platform, while WD 0-6-0ST 75171 prepares to take water, having arrived from Abbey station, Shrewsbury with the daily 'civilian' goods train. The time is the summer of 1949.

BELOW: The last order of steam to work to Llanfyllin, Ivatt designed and Swindon built BR Class 2 2-6-0 46506, arrives at Llanymynech with the branch train on 2 May 1956. Even at this late date Cambrian signals still dominate the scene at the south junction in the distance, the nameboard still advises "CHANGE FOR LLANFYLLIN AND LAKE VYRNWY" — a long walk! — and the first class refreshment room still occupies the up platform; there was also a second (3rd class) for lesser mortals.

ABOVE: As might be expected, the Llanfyllin branch came very low down on Dr Beeching's list of priorities but an earlier economy was effected when Llanymynech Junction South was completely re-modelled in 1954. Both the double junctions on the S&MR and Llanfyllin line were converted to single lines, thereby simplifying the layout and forcing trains bound for the branch to cross over to the up Cambrian main line.

RIGHT: A rare view of Llanfyllin Branch Junction in September 1937. The 'new' curve to Llanfyllin (opened 21 January 1896) veers to the left away from the unlifted stub of the former Potteries, Shrewsbury and North Wales Blodwell and Nantmawr quarry line (used for wagon storage at this time). The Blodwell Junction section had been worked by the Cambrian for goods trains from 1 June 1881 and for passenger traffic from 5 January 1904. Unfortunately, this service between Llanymynech and Blodwell Junction only lasted until 1 January 1917, leaving a single daily freight; even this expired in 1925, after which the rails were recovered north of Rhydmeredydd. This view from the B4398 road at Wern, overlooks the Shropshire Union Canal aqueduct, in effect a double bridge over the railway. Carreghofa Halt, opened by the GWR on 11th April 1938 on a site fifty yards to the east of the bridge came seven months after this photograph was taken. *Photo: the late R. K. Cope*

Llanymynech — Llanfyllin

RIGHT: Llansantffraid, the only crossing station on the branch and the most important intermediate stop. GWR 74XX Class 0-6-0PT 7410 arrives with the 1.25 pm train from Llanfyllin on 10 May 1956. The signal box on the down side has an adjacent crossing loop from which a connection gave access to an extensive yard with large warehouse and goods shed. The original formation of the branch from Llanymynech as far as Llansantffraid allowed for double track.

BELOW: The terminus at Llanfyllin was quite substantial, with a run-round loop and a single platform dominated by a large Victorian building. In addition, the large yard contained a warehouse, freight shed, locomotive shed and water tower together with cattle pens — sheep and lambs always formed a substantial source of traffic. GWR 7410 waits to depart for Oswestry with the 1.25 pm train. The 74XX 0-6-0PT were introduced to the line in 1936.

Llanymynech — Llanfyllin

Five years earlier, in 1951, GWR 0-4-2T 5812 arrives at the terminus with the twin-set. While shedded at Oswestry this locomotive spent a large part of its waking life shuttling to and from Llanfyllin and also Llangynog on the beautiful Tanat Valley line.
Photo: R. C. Riley

LLANFYLLIN BRANCH.

Down Trains. Week Days only.

Mile Post Mileage.		Miles from Oswestry.		STATIONS.		Ruling Gradient 1 in	Time Allowances for Freight Trains. See page 2.			B Pass.	G Light Engine WO	B Pass.		K Goods W8X	K Goods W8O	B Pass. W8O		B Pass.		B Pass.	B Auto ex Gobowen.	B Pass. WO	B Pass. SO	B Pass. SO	
							Point to Point Times.	Allow for Stop.	Allow for Start.																
M.	C.	M.	C.				Mins.	Mins.	Mins.	a.m.	a.m.	a.m.		p.m.	p.m.	p.m.		p.m.		p.m.	p.m.	p.m.	p.m.	p.m.	
—	—	5	78	LLANYMYNECH	dep.	50 R. & F.	....	....	1	8 33	9 12	11 13	....	12 25	12X19	1 13	..	3X44	....	5 25	6 30	9 24	9 30	11 25	....
—	—	6	7	cLlanymynech J. Sth.	,,	....	....	..	..	8 36	—	11 16	....	—	—	1 16	...	3 47	....	5 28	6 33	9 27	9·33	11 28	
—	58	6	65	Carreghofa Halt	,,	....	....	..	..	—	—	9 14		—	—	—		—		—	—	—	—	—	
—	61	6	68	Llanfyllin B. Junction	,,	....	9	1	..	8 41½	X9‖20	1121½	....	12 36	12 30	1 21½	..	3 52½	....	5 33½	6 38½	9 32½	9 38½	1133½	
3	7	9	14	cLlansantffraid ...... { arr.		....	....		1	8 42½	9‖27	11 23	....	1 5	12 50	1 23		3 54		5 35	6 40	9 34	9 40	11 35	
				{ dep.			..	..																	
4	64	10	71	Llanfechain .... { arr.		75 R.	6	1		8 47	—	1127½	....	ST	ST	1 27½		3 58½		5 39½	6 44½	9 38½	9 44½	11 40	
				{ dep.			..	..	1	8 52½	—	11 33				1 33		4 4		5 45	6 50	9 44	9 50	11 46	
6	53	12	60	Bryngwyn	,,	77 R.	..	..																	
8	41	14	48	cLLANFYLLIN	arr.	221 R.	11	1	....	8 57½	9‖45	11 38	....	1 35	1 15	1 38		4 9		5 50	6 55	9 49	9 55	11 51	

Up Trains. Week Days only.

Miles from Llanfyllin.		STATIONS.		Ruling Gradient 1 in	Time Allowances for Freight Trains. See page 2.			B Pass.	B Pass. WO	B Pass.	B Pass. W8O	B Pass.	K Goods	B Pass.	B Auto.	D Empty Train. WO	B Pass. SO	D Empty Train. SO
					Point to Point Times.	Allow for Stop.	Allow for Start.											
M.	C.				Mins.	Mins.	Mins.	a.m.	a.m.	a.m.	a.m.	p.m.	p.m.	p.m.	p.m.	p.m.	p.m.	p.m.
—	—	cLLANFYLLIN	dep.	221 F.	....	....	1	7 23	9 5	10 25	11 55	1 43	2 30	4 28	7 30	7‡45	8 25	10†10
1	68	Bryngwyn	,,	..	....	....	..	7 28	9 10	10 30	1159½	1 47½		4 33	7 34½	—	8 30	—
					..	..			9 14									
3	57	Llanfechain .... { arr.		77 F.	8	1		7 33	9§18	10 35	12 4	1 52	CR	4 38	7 39	—	8 35	—
		{ dep.			..	..	1	7 37	9 22	10 39	12 8	1 56	3 0	4 42	7 43	—	8 39	—
5	34	cLlansantffraid ...... { arr.		75 F.	4	1		7 38	9X§28	10 40	12 8½	1 57	3 30	4 43	7 44	—	8 40	—
		{ dep.			..	..	1											
7	60	Llanfyllin B. Junction	,,	..	..	..			9 31				—					
7	63	Carreghofa Halt	,,	..	..	..	..	7 44½	9†34½	1046½	12 15	2 3½	—	4 49½	7 50½	—	—	—
8	41	cLlanymynech J. Sth.	,,	..	9	1	..											
8	50	LLANYMYNECH	arr.	50 R. & F.				7 47	9 37	10 49	12X17½	2 6	3X42	4 52	7 53	8† 10	8 47	10†30

§—Advertised 3 minutes earlier. ‡—Advertised 9.32 a.m.

Abermule~Kerry

The steeply graded Kerry Railway, promoted largely by local interests, lost its identity within four months of its inauguration, when the Cambrian Railways Company came into existence in July 1864, swallowing up four constituents in the process including the Oswestry and Newtown. For sixty-seven years the railway provided transport facilities for the thinly populated uplands via the Kerry railhead, although the station itself was still a mile from the village it purported to serve. Both village and station lay on the A489, Newtown-Craven Arms road. Farm produce and livestock, especially sheep, timber and bricks, went down the hill through the steep sided, twisting valley and gorge of the river Mule to the main line station at Abermule, in exchange for coal, lime, fertilisers and groceries. The fact that the line rarely needed the services of more than one passenger coach is indicative of its relatively weak geographical position in relation to local traffic flows; this was its downfall. To reach the major market town of Newtown required a roundabout journey and a good deal of patience. No wonder the direct bus service to Newtown market introduced in 1930 killed off the passenger service in 1931, when GWR economies closed the Kerry, Mawddwy and Llanfair Caereinion lines at a stroke. The freight service survived, latterly on three or two days a week for another quarter of a century and because of locomotive working restrictions the last two surviving Dean Goods 0-6-0s, 2516 and 2538, both based at Oswestry, worked out their last years on the branch freights.

LEFT: 2516 shunts Kerry yard on one of its thrice weekly forays along the branch, the load is four empty coal wagons and one loaded with wooden pit props. The locomotive shed, closed in 1931, still exists today, now converted to a hay barn.

ORIGINS:	The Kerry Railway (Oswestry and Newtown Railway Act 1861)
LENGTH:	3m 61ch
OPENED:	2 March 1863
CLOSED:	9 February 1931 (Passengers) 1 May 1956 (Freight)
RULING GRADIENT:	1 in 43

Welshpool

ABERMULE

Newtown

Fronfraith
1m 28c

Goitre
Siding
2m 29c

N

KERRY
3m 61c   Kerry
Tramway

ABOVE: On a bitterly cold day in December 1955, the driver of GWR Dean goods 0-6-0 2516 gets the 'right away' from the guard at Kerry. The yellow GW style buffer beam number is a reminder that 2516 was in much demand for hauling enthusiast rail tours at this time. Happily she is still with us, tucked up warm and dry in Swindon Museum.

KERRY BRANCH.

DOWN TRAINS.   **WEEK DAYS ONLY.**

Mile Post Mileage.	STATIONS.		Ruling Gradient 1 in	Point-to Point Times.	Allow for Stop.	Allow for Start.		K Goods W Th SO	K Goods MO	
M. C.				Mins.	Mins.	Mins.		a.m.	a.m.	
— 10	*a*Abermule	dep.	75 R.	....	..	1	...	9 30	11 30	...
1 28	Fronfraith	,,		13	1	1	...	— CR	— CR	...
2 29	Goitre Siding	,,	43 R.	8	1	1	...	10 15	12 15	...
3 61	*a*Kerry	arr.	..				...			...

UP TRAINS.   **WEEK DAYS ONLY.**

Miles from Kerry.	STATIONS.		Ruling Gradient 1 in	Point to Point Times.	Allow for Stop.	Allow for Start.		K Goods W Th SO	K Goods MO	
M. C.				Mins.	Mins.	Mins.		a.m.	p.m.	
—	*a*Kerry	dep.		....	....	1	...	11 15	12 45	...
— 58½	Stop Board	,,					...	P	—	...
1 32	Goitre Siding	,,	43 F.	8	1	1	...	—	—	...
2 33	Fronfraith	,,					...	CR	—	...
3 51	*a*Abermule	arr.	75 F.	13	1	1	...	12 0	1 30	...

Branch worked by one engine in steam.
The speed allowed for running on the Kerry Branch is under no circumstances to be exceeded.

A wider angle 1952 photograph gives a much better impression of the size of the spacious layout in the station yard at Kerry: run-round loop (left), four long sidings and a spur to the locomotive shed. Dean goods 0-6-0 2411 stands at the platform waiting to work an outward bound sheep special; the internationally famous Kerry Hill sheep sales were held near the village on the first and third Fridays in September every year.

A steam operated 'two foot' (1′ 11½″) gauge tramway for the carriage of timber connected Kerry station to afforested land on the estate of Brynllywarch Hall in the early 1890s, when there were over five miles of track including branches. The tramway closed in 1895 but was resuscitated between 1917 and 1922 at the instigation of the Board of Trade, the Estate, and the War Department. A German prisoner of war camp, sited nearby, provided a large proportion of the work force.

ABOVE: Two very different stages in the life of Kerry station house:
Left, from the buffer stops looking north east in 1954. The cattle pens on the right were heavily used during the sheep sales period. The locomotive shed is visible (far left).
Right, re-furbished as a desirable private residence as it appeared in the summer of 1985. The derelict and decaying brick weighbridge house can just be detected under the trees in the distance. *Photo: Andrew Bannister*

RIGHT: Goitre was the more notherly of the two intermediate stations (halts!) on the Kerry branch, 2¼ miles from Abermule. A trailing connection on the downside formed a siding which served Goitre brickworks, a valuable source of revenue for the line up to the second world war. The railway here climbs on a punishing gradient of 1 in 43 for nearly a mile, the steepest worked by standard gauge passenger trains on the whole of the Cambrian Railways system.

Abermule — Kerry

Abermule — Kerry

ABOVE: 2538 with its lightweight load is posed for a photograph near Goitre by a helpful driver, only one month before the Kerry branch closed for good. Goitre platform and siding lie beyond the brakevan while the brickworks chimney dominates the scene of the eastern side.

RIGHT: Fronfraith looking down the gorge of the river Mule. The facing siding thrown off on the 'down' side once served the mill and the diminutive platform was only twenty seven feet long. Both are difficult to identify in this 1955 photograph.

LEFT: The Kerry Hill sheep sales on Friday 19 September 1952 required the services of only one special train. Dean goods 0-6-0 2411 already gets to grips with the rising gradient as it leaves the Kerry bay at Abermule with the empty stock. Unfortunately road transporters had usurped most of the livestock traffic by this time.

BELOW: Special traffic on the Kerry branch requires extra staff and accompanying officialdom. Sporting a brake van at each end of the train, GWR Dean goods 0-6-0 2411 and seven cattle wagons arrive at the terminus prior to loading sheep from the Kerry Sales. Empty pens on the cattle dock await the woolly customers from the show ground up the road towards Kerry village on this uncharacteristically cold September day in 1952.

Cemmes Road~ Dinas Mawddwy

This independent, poverty stricken and rather remote railway was promoted and largely paid for by Sir Edmund Buckley, lord of the manor. He was also responsible for the construction of the 1′ 11″ gauge Hendre-ddu Tramway, a narrow gauge feeder line for slate traffic. Carriage of farm produce, livestock, timber, coal but mainly slate from the local quarries in the Dovey Valley, formed the basis of its existence, coupled with a meagre revenue from passenger traffic. Hitherto local slate had to be carried on pack horses to the sea at Aberdovey on the Cardigan Bay coast.

The Mawddwy Railway belonged to that small group of lines in Britain that had the distinction of opening and closing twice. By 1900 the gross receipts amounted to less than £1,500 and passenger services were terminated in the following year. The line continued its penurous existence until 1908 when even the meagre freight service gave up the ghost, the track being too feeble to sustain it.

Nowadays one can only view the confidence and enterprise of some of the Victorian railway entrepreneurs with astonishment and admiration for, within three years the Mawddwy rose like the proverbial phoenix and re-opened under the auspices of a Light Railway Order, some financial help from the government and a massive cash injection from David Davies, then chairman of the Cambrian Railway Company and grandson of the eminent David Davies of Llandinam, Welsh railway promoter and contractor *extraordinaire*. The Cambrian agreed to reconstruct the Mawddwy and work the line for seventy per cent of the receipts. It was a forlorn hope. The line never came anywhere near to prosperity, in fact it never paid a single dividend to its shareholders in the eighty-three years of its existence. When the Great Western Railway takeover came in 1922, the Mawddwy hung like a millstone round its neck. 1931 signified the end of passenger services for a second time; the Corris and Kerry lines went simultaneously with the Welshpool and Llanfair to follow a month later.

Death came abruptly and without warning in the September of 1951, not from a stroke of the British Rail chief accountant's pen but by a freak of nature,

ORIGINS:	Mawddwy Railway (Mawddwy Railway Act 1865)
LENGTH:	6m 63ch
OPENED:	1 October 1867
CLOSED:	17 April 1901 (Freight 8 April 1908)
RE-OPENED:	29 July 1911
CLOSED:	1 January 1931 (Freight 1 July 1951). Last freight train ran 5 September 1950
RULING GRADIENT:	1 in 41

when an in spate River Dovey seriously weakened the Railway bridge to the north of Cemmaes station. Significantly, the angry Dovey proved instrumental in closing two of its railways within three years as the Corris had already been eliminated in 1948. By May 1952 a contractor from Sheffield had lifted the mortal remains of the Mawddwy, the only hardware left behind being Dinas station and locomotive shed, now restored and converted for use as a tea room and pottery.

LEFT: The short platform at Mallwyd, 5¾ miles from Cemmes Road, once possessed a waiting shed but no siding. Lewis Cozens described the valley of the Dovey hereabouts as being "particularly beautiful with the river flowing through a rocky gorge with falls at nearby Pen-y-bont". Pictured here in 1951 the station had not witnessed a regular passenger train for twenty years, in fact the only passenger stock to work over the branch was the combined Dovey Valley Sunday Schools' excursion to Aberystwyth run annually in June and which last operated in 1939.

ABOVE: First station of the branch from Cemmes Road and 1½ miles from the Cambrian main line, Cemmaes lay on a rising gradient of 1 in 83. The first photograph was taken on 13 August 1951, facing north, and illustrates the ground frame and siding on the approach side of the platform.

The second view looks south to Cemmes Road across the river Dovey. The bridge in the foreground was instrumental in finally closing the Dinas Mawddwy branch in 1950. The unpredictable moods of the river on several occasions in previous years had caused temporary cessation of services on the line. During the demolition of the track in 1952 the bridge had to be specially shored up to allow the passage of Dean goods 0-6-0 2323.

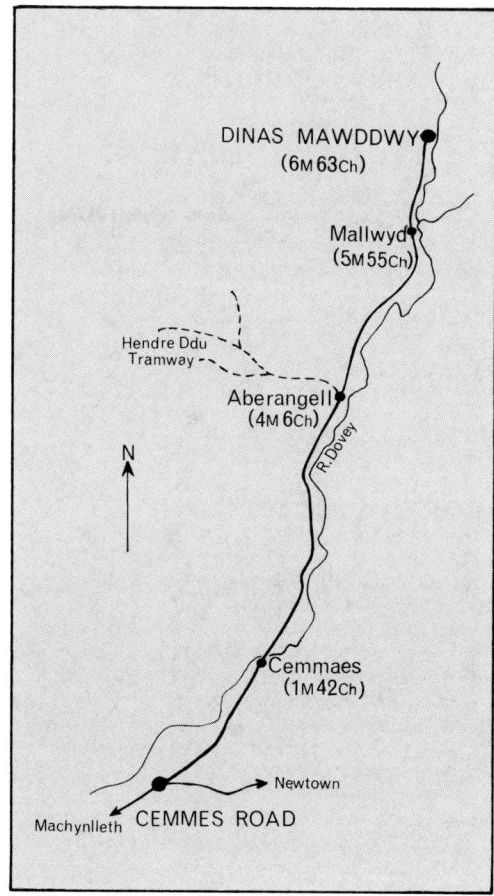

MAWDDWY BRANCH. Week Days only.

	DOWN TRAINS.			K		UP TRAINS.			K
M.P. Mileage.	STATIONS.		Ruling Gradient.	Goods MW FO	M.P. Mileage.	STATIONS.		Ruling Gradient.	Goods MW FO
M.	C.			a.m.	M.	C.			a.m.
—	—	aDinas Mawddwy ...... dep.		10 50	—	—	Machynlleth ...... dep.		9 0
1	8	Mallwyd ...... ,,	120 F.	—	—	1	Cemmes Road {arr. dep.		9 18 9 38
2	57	Aberangell ...... {arr. dep.	51 F.	CR			Cemmes {arr. dep.	41 F.	ST
5	21	Cemmaes ...... {arr. dep.	100 F.	CR	1	42	Aberangell ...... {arr. dep.	100 R.	CR
6	62	acCemmes Road ...... {arr. dep.	41 R.	11 20 11 39	4	6	Mallwyd ...... ,,	51 R.	—
—	—	cMachynlleth ...... arr.		11 55	5	55	Dinas Mawddwy ...... arr.	120 R.	10 10
					6	63			

Branch worked by one engine in steam.

DINAS MAWDDWY (6M 63Ch)

Mallwyd (5M 55Ch)

Hendre Ddu Tramway

Aberangell (4M 6Ch)

R. Dovey

N

Cemmaes (1M 42Ch)

Newtown

Machynlleth   CEMMES ROAD

RIGHT: Aberangell station, viewed towards the south on 13 August 1951, was the terminus of the narrow gauge tramway from Hendre-ddu quarry. Slate was brought down to the transhipment platform adjoining the south end of the Mawddwy railway freight siding. This siding was connected to the 'main line' at each end forming a loop, which, according to GWR instructions, was for 'emergency use only' and 'worked under proper authority'.

BELOW: GWR 824 formerly Mawddwy Railway 0-6-0ST *Mawddwy* built by Manning Wardle in 1864. It worked the Van branch until closure in 1940. *Photo: Colling Turner*

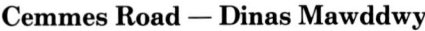

Cemmes Road — Dinas Mawddwy

BOTTOM:
Two views of auto-fitted GWR 0-4-2T 1434 awaiting departure from the terminus as Dinas Mawddwy on 24 September 1948 with the 1.45 pm service to Cemmes Road.

Two years before final closure the freight service operated on Tuesdays and Fridays only, and then 'as required', calls being made at Cemmaes and Aberangell if necessary. The branch, worked on the 'one engine in steam' principle, was unsignalled and trains were limited to a maximum speed of 25 mph. During the period of Great Western ownership a heterogeneous collection of locomotives could be observed wandering along the grass-grown byways of Merioneth and Montgomeryshire, the Mawddwy line being no exception. Class 517, Wolverhampton built 0-4-2Ts and their Collett successors of the 4800 (later 1400) and 5800 classes, rubbed shoulders with the fascinating little Cambrian Railway Sharp Stewart 2-4-0 tanks and ex-Lambourn Valley Railway 0-6-0 tank 819. GW 846 lasted not only to the end of the Mawddwy passenger services but was not cut up at Swindon until 1946. 824, the original *Mawddwy* built by Manning Wardle in 1864 was quickly put out to grass (quite literally!) on the Van lead mines branch at Caersws, lasting until 1940.

The mood of the late September weather depicted in the photograph reflects the run down appearance of the scene at Dinas Mawddwy with very little traffic on offer and an unkempt station yard. Beyond the brakevan on the extreme right of the picture lie the goods and locomotive sheds while the station is almost totally obscured by the trees in the distance. Twenty four months to go! *Photo: the late R. K. Cope per R. S. Carpenter*

Lampeter~ Aberayron

ORIGINS:	Lampeter, Aberayron and New Quay Light Railway
LENGTH:	12m 14ch (1m 24ch Lampeter-Aberayron Junction)
OPENED:	12 May 1911
CLOSED:	7 May 1951 (Passenger)
	5 April 1965 (Freight: Green Grove Siding-Aberayron)
	30 September 1973 (Freight: Green Grove Siding-Aberayron Jct)
RULING GRADIENT:	1 in 40

BELOW: Bathed in late afternoon sunshine GWR 74XX 0-6-0PT 7402 waits at Aberayron to work the 4.40 pm train to Green Grove Siding and Lampeter on 24 August 1956. Traces of flat bottomed track are evident in the run-round loop, a reminder that the line was originally built to light railway standards.

Lampeter — Aberayron

ABOVE: The single platform terminus at Aberayron on 28 August 1956, still open for freight and parcels traffic five years after the cessation of passenger traffic in 1951. The yard facilities consisted of a run-round loop, three parallel sidings, a trailing connection leading to a single road locomotive shed, cattle pens and standing crane. Behind the line of wagons lie two goods sheds, one constructed in concrete as late as 1956 as a grain store. At this time three trains operated daily between Aberayron and Lampeter; a branch freight and two milk services.

Until 1951 the Index of Stations in Bradshaw's Railway Guide contained an entry for New Quay and how many prospective holidaymakers ended the journey by motor bus in Cardiganshire rather than by rail to Cornwall is a matter of speculation, after all, both were seaside holiday resorts blessed with superb sandy beaches, but the Welsh New Quay never got its station. A footnote in Bradshaw reads "Aberayron — station for New Quay — 7½ miles". For the aspiring passenger (or should it be perspiring?) Bradshaw offered another footnote gem in the Newcastle Emlyn branch table, — "Llandyssul — station for New Quay, 16 miles". The famous Bradshaw pointed finger symbol provided a further rejoinder, "A Service of Road Motors runs between Llandyssul and New Quay".

If plans had materialised New Quay was supposed to have had its own station. The line got no further than Aberayron but bore a grandiose title, the 'Lampeter, Aberayron and New Quay Light Railway Company'. Never paying a dividend to shareholders in its whole life, the LA and NQLR was worked by the GWR from the beginning but retained its independence until absorbed in 1923. Preceding the official opening in 1911, the GWR, never slow off the mark, had operated a road motor service between Aberayron and Lampeter for five years.

Two of David Davies' early schemes for linking Aberayron with the outside world by rail foundered between 1860 and 1880, as did a plan to extend the Vale of Rheidol narrow gauge from Aberystwyth and a Cambrian scheme to build from Llanrhystyd Road station. From the beginning of the nineteenth century Aberayron had developed a small harbour into a busy port for coastal trade, importing manufactured goods, coal and fertilisers and sending out agricultural produce and minerals from a hinterland fringed by a mountain barrier and devoid of adequate transport facilities, the Manchester and Milford Railway not reaching Aberystwyth by way of Lampeter until 1867.

The opening of a railway to Aberayron spelt eventual death for the port trade, the carriage of coal being particularly affected. The gradual silting up of the harbour and the declining coastal trade hastened closure in the mid-nineteen thirties. The Aberayron

Steam Packet Company Ltd had been wound up as early as 1917. The turn of the railway came on 10th February 1951, a temporary closure during the coal shortage of that winter was confirmed permanently three months later. Freight traffic lingered for a brief period on the western half of the line but the eastern section received a shot in the arm when the Milk Marketing Board constructed a new factory at Green Grove, a mile west of Felin Fach — at least part of the branch was to enjoy another twenty-two years of useful existence.

BELOW: The original locomotive shed at Aberayron, which lay some distance east of the station, was replaced in 1926, when an ex-Cambrian Railways corrugated iron structure was retrieved from Wrexham and re-erected. This view was taken on 28 August 1956. Although a sub-shed of Machynlleth (89C), Aberayron branch locomotives were maintained at Carmarthen after passenger services ceased in 1951, a 74XX class pannier tank being exchanged weekly. From the beginning of 1961 Aberayron was transferred as a sub-shed to Carmarthen (87G), closing finally in February 1962. The trailing connection from the loop to the locomotive shed threw off a short spur serving the coal stage.

LAMPETER AND ABERAYRON.

SINGLE LINE WORKED BY ELECTRIC TRAIN STAFF.

Sections.	Crossing Station.
Lampeter and Felin Fach	Felin Fach.
Felin Fach and Aberayron	Aberayron.

Down Trains. Week Days.

Mile Post Mileage.	Distance from Lampeter.	STATIONS.	B Auto. arr.	B Auto. dep.	K Carmarthen Junction Goods. arr.	K Carmarthen Junction Goods. dep.	B Auto. arr.	B Auto. dep.	B Auto. arr.	B Auto. dep.	B N Auto. SX arr.	B N Auto. SX dep.	B Auto. arr.	B Auto. dep.
M.C.	M.C.		A.M.	A.M.	A.M.	A.M.	A.M.	A.M.	P.M.	P.M.	P.M.	P.M.	P.M.	P.M.
— —		Lampeter	7 57	8 15	7 40	8 55	10 57	11 25	2 12	3 40	....	...	6 37	7 5
— —	1 24	Aberayron J.		8 19		9 0		11 29		3 44	....	...		7 9
—45	1 69	Silian Halt	—	8 22	C R		—	11 32	—	3 47	....	...	—	7 12
2 49½	3 73¼	Stop Board			C P						....	...		
2 61	4 5	Blaenplwyf H.	—	8 30			—	11 40	—	3 55	...	...	—	7 20
4 49	5 73	Talsarn Halt	—	8 37	S T		—	11 47	—	4 2	...	...	—	7 27
4 51	5 75	Stop Board			S P						...	...		
6 58	7 2	Stop Board			P						...	...		
6 0	7 24	Felin Fach	8 42	8 43	9 30	10 30	11 52	11 53	4 7	4 9	—	5 0	7 32	7 33
8 44	9 68	Ciliau Aeron	—	8 51	C R		—	12 1	—	4 17	—	5 8	—	7 41
9 37	10 61	Crossways H.	—	8 55			—	12 5	—	4 21	—	5 12	—	7 45
9 64	11 8	Stop Board			P									
10 28	11 52	Ll'n'rch'y'r'nH	—	8 59			—	12 9	—	4 25	—	5 16	—	7 49
12 14	13 38	Aberayron	9 5	10 5	11 0	11 20	12 15	1 20	4 31		5 22		7 55	

Up Trains. Week Days

Distance from Aberayron.	STATIONS.	B Auto. arr.	B Auto. dep.	B Auto. arr.	B Auto. dep.	K Goods to Carmarthen Junction. arr.	K Goods to Carmarthen Junction. dep.	B Auto. arr.	B Auto. dep.	B N Auto. SX arr.	B N Auto. SX dep.	B Auto. arr.	B Auto. dep.
M.C.		A.M.	A.M.	A.M.	A.M.	A.M.	A.M.	P.M.	P.M.	P.M.	P.M.	P.M.	P.M.
	Aberayron ..		7 5	9 5	10 5	11 0	11 20	12 15	1 20		4 35		5 45
1 66	Llanerchayron Halt		7 11	—	10 11	—		—	1 26	—	4 41	—	5 51
2 57	Crossways Halt	—	7 15	—	10 15	—		—	1 30	—	4 45	—	5 55
3 50	Ciliau Aeron ..	—	7 20	—	10 20	11 36	11 40	—	1 35	—	4 50	—	6 0
6 14	Felin Fach	7 27	7 28	10 27	10 28	11 50	12 35	1 42	1 43	4 57	—	6 7	6 8
7 46	Talsarn Halt ..	—	7 35	—	10 35	S T		—	1 50	...	...	—	6 15
9 33	Blaenplwyf Halt ..	—	7 43	—	10 43	P		—	1 58	...	...	—	6 23
9 54	Stop Board ..					P							
11 43	Stop Board												
11 49	Silian Halt ..	—	7 51	—	10 51			—	2 6	...	...	—	6 31
14	Aberayron Junction		7 53		10 53		1 10		2 9				6 33
13 38	Lampeter	7 57	8 15	10 57	11 25	1 15	1 55	2 12	3 40			6 37	7 5

The level crossings are provided with Cattle Guards and a white post is fixed alongside the Railway, at a distance of 300 yards on each side of the crossing. Trains and engines must not exceed a speed of 10 miles per hour, between each notice board and the crossing, and must be prepared to stop dead before fouling each crossing. The figure "10" appears on each post as an indication of this speed restriction.

N Will not run when schools are closed.

ABOVE: GWR 0-6-0PT 7402 with the 4.40 pm train from Aberayron to Green Grove Siding, makes a vigorous attack on the short pitch of 1 in 63 between Ciliau Aeron and Felin Fach on 28 August 1956. At Green Grove Creamery, London bound tankers will be collected for attachment at Carmarthen to the evening milk train. The 120 yard long loop line and ground frame at Green Grove opened on 1 October 1951, the new milk traffic offering some compensation for the loss in passenger revenue the same year.

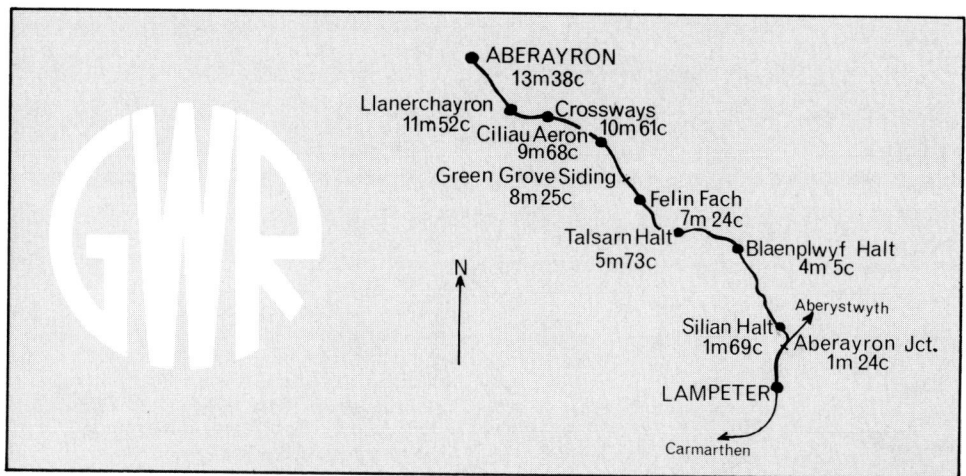

ABERAYRON
13m 38c

Llanerchayron
11m 52c

Crossways
10m 61c

Ciliau Aeron
9m 68c

Green Grove Siding
8m 25c

Felin Fach
7m 24c

Talsarn Halt
5m 73c

Blaenplwyf Halt
4m 5c

N

Aberystwyth

Silian Halt
1m 69c

Aberayron Jct.
1m 24c

LAMPETER

Carmarthen

Lampeter — Aberayron

Also on 28 August 1956, the 5.15 pm milk train from Green Grove to Lampeter pulls into Felin Fach behind GWR 0-6-0PT 7402, the two milk tanks bound for West Ealing. Situated halfway, and the most important intermediate station on the branch, Felin Fach (originally Ystrad for two years) boasted the only crossing loop and two platforms.

Constructed under the provisions of the Light Railway Act the Aberayron railway was originally laid with flat bottomed track, maximum speed being limited to 25 mph. This speed was further reduced to 10 mph over the twelve ungated crossings on the branch.

Bala Jcn~ Blaenau Festiniog

ORIGINS:	**Festiniog and Blaenau Railway (1′ 11½″), Bala and Festiniog Railway**
LENGTH:	**25m 35ch**
OPENED:	**(1) 30 May 1868 Festiniog-Duffws**
	(2) 1 November 1882 Bala Junction-Bala
	(3) 10 September 1883 Bala-Festiniog
CLOSED:	**Bala-Blaenau Festiniog 4 January 1960 (Freight 28 January 1961)**
RE-OPENED:	**Blaenau Festiniog-Trawsfynydd CEGB Siding 20 April 1964**
RULING GRADIENT:	**1 in 50**

ABOVE: Bala station in May 1957 looking south towards Bala Junction. Constructed in 1882 by the Bala and Festiniog Railway, the station replaced the original structure of the Corwen and Bala Railway built in 1868, and was very much nearer the town centre. The double track section to the junction was operated as two separate single lines; the downside platform, being more accessible, catered for both the Bala Junction shuttle and trains for Blaenau Festiniog. For the whole of its existence the junction remained one of those interesting GWR interchange stations situated amid fields and having no road access, very similar to Dovey Junction. There was no booking office, indeed the station even failed to materialise in public timetables. Bala station possessed a locomotive shed (1882-1965), a turntable hidden behind the signal box and generous freight facilities, the most prominent feature being a large stone built and castellated goods depot capable of accomodating over thirty wagons. GWR 0-6-0PT 7414 has just left its single coach at the down platform before running round and returning with the next service to Blaenau Festiniog.

The Great Western branch from the shores of Bala Lake (Llyn Tegid) to the sterile landscape of Blaenau Festiniog has not received the attention it merits and any description must use frequent superlatives. There were few lines in England and Wales, where, for much of the distance, the countryside was so comprehensively desolate and uninviting. In twelve miles or so from the wooded softer landscape around Bala, (530′ above sea level) it climbed up 750′ through and finally over the mountainous terrain of the Arenig Ranges, occupied only by dispersed small communities, isolated farmsteads and sheep. The gradients were not only long and fearsome but awkward into the bargain, and the tendency to excessive moisture in the region for much of the year proved a positive hindrance. The higher of the railway's two summits at Cwm Prysor (1,278′), spent many days of the year shrouded in mist, cloud and drizzle when it wasn't actually raining, no doubt it kept the fishermen at nearby Llyn Treweryn very happy.

The lower lands of the Treweryn valley between Bala and Frongoch offered some agricultural employment, but apart from the arrival of the Forestry Commission after the first world war the only real industry involved mineral extraction in the form of granite from Arenig — once described as "the most desolate station on the GWR" — and slate from Llan Festiniog, Manod and Blaenau Festiniog. The latter was the 'raison d'etre' behind the construction of the Bala and Festiniog, opened in 1882, and very much a latecomer in the field for the great years of the slate trade had passed their zenith. "Slate direct to Birmingham and the industrial Midland towns" was the call, a route hardly more direct than the customary outlets but just as competitive. The narrow gauge Festiniog Railway carried the bulk of the quarried slate and had been operating to Portmadoc since 1832, supplemented in 1868 by the Festiniog and Blaenau Railway also 1′ 11½″ gauge (later converted to standard) which made its line from the FR at Dwffws to Llan Festiniog, 3½ miles distant. Throughout its existence under the aegis of the GWR (later BR Western Region) traffic on the branch never reached the levels projected. Except on Saturdays passenger trains rarely required the services of more than one brake composite coach and an 0-6-0PT or 0-4-2T locomotive. Military trains to and from Trawsfynydd with traffic for the gunnery ranges were a different matter, in fact they could be quite exciting when larger engines were allocated to work a heavy load over this difficult route, assisted from Bala by a banker. In 1939, 78XX 4-6-0s of the Manor class, 26XX Aberdare 2-6-0s and 51XX 2-6-2T engines were allowed to work troop trains up from Ruabon via Bala Junction at a speed not exceeding 20 mph over the branch and Churchward 43XX 2-6-0s had been added to the list by 1950. The Working Timetable Appendix instructed that "assistant engines must be placed in front of troop trains." The twisting, steep and tightly curved section north of Trawsfynydd, especially over the formation of the original Festiniog and Blaenau Railway was always restricted to 'Yellow' and 'Uncoloured Group' engines of the 0-6-0T and 0-4-2T types, but it must have been a discouraging business working a troop train down the hill from Trawsfynydd to Bala running tender first in bad weather, as there were no turning facilities at the military station.

Most of the line was closed between 1960 and 1961, yet another victim of Welsh water, this time contained by artificial means when the valley between Arenig and Frongoch was flooded by Liverpool Corporation under the Treweryn Valley (Llyn Celyn) scheme authorised in 1957. The last freight from Ruabon ran on 27 January 1961 behind GWR 0-6-0PT 9752. There had been a proposal to deviate the line for two miles at a cost of £1.1 million but BR decided to close the branch on the understanding that a new connection from the LNWR Conway Valley line would be made at Blaenau Festiniog. This was duly completed and opened on 20th April 1964. The branch still operates to a point about one and a quarter miles north of Trawsfynydd station where a siding has been laid to serve Trawsfynydd nuclear power station. A weekly freight train carrying flasks of atomic waste for re-processing runs to British Nuclear Fuels at Sellafield in Cumbria by way of Blaenau, Bettws-y-Coed and Llandudno Junction.

ABOVE: GWR 0-6-0PT 8791 pauses at Frongoch on 9 May 1957 with the 9.15 am Blaenau Festiniog-Bala service. Two and a half miles from Bala the single platform served the small village lying adjacent on the A4212 Bala-Trawsfynydd road. The signal box contained the lever frame while the electric train token instrument was situated in the booking office. In the distance at the north end lay a small yard and goods shed. North of Frongoch the landscape became progressively wilder as the railway continued to climb towards Arenig. In between lay stopping places at Tyddyn Bridge and Capel Celyn created by the GWR as halts in 1931. This section was to disappear when the artificially created Llyn Celyn inundated the valley after 1961.

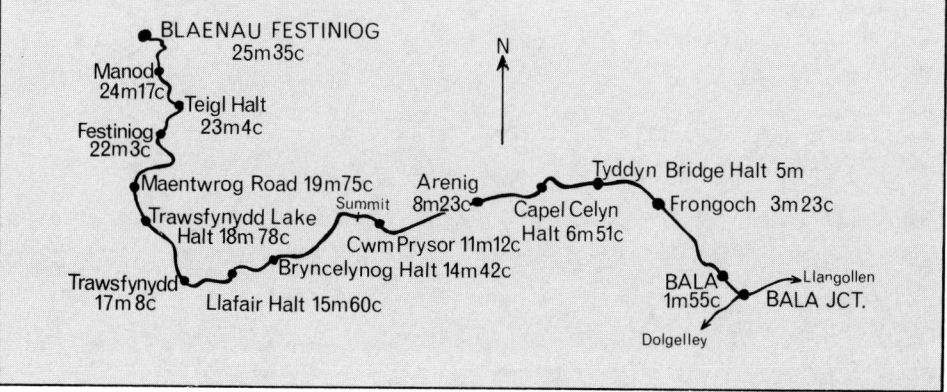

RIGHT: Arenig station and passing loop from the south in 1955. Seven and a half miles from Bala and over eleven hundred feet above sea level, Arenig lay very close to the tree line. The Arenig Granite Company's crushing plant and sidings were situated at the north end with an overhead conveyor carrying the quarried stone across the line. The close proximity of the quarry required special precautions when blasting was due to take place, the quarry company giving written notice to the Arenig station master one hour before blasting and displaying red and green flags accordingly. In the later years Arenig quarry provided large quantities of ballast for BR. On the steep and twisting mountain section between Frongoch and Trawsfynydd there were a number of "Permanent Restriction of Speed boards fitted with long-burning lamps which will be left burning night and day." Such was the importance attached to these boards that fogmen, equipped with lamps, flags and detonators were appointed to man each one "in falling snow or fog".

LEFT: A scene full of interest for the railway modeller with trains crossing at Arenig on 2 May 1957. GWR 0-6-0PT 7442, heading north with the 9.35 am freight from Bala, takes water while 7443 prepares to depart with the 9.15 am pasenger from Blaenau Festiniog. Operating the branch at high altitudes in the winter months brought inevitable problems with the weather, and instructions regarding Snow Storms figured largely in the Appendix to the Working Timetables. "The state of the line during snow storms must be fully advised by telegram to the station master at Bala .... if there is likely to be a block he must report by wire to the Divisional Engineer Shrewsbury, Divisional Locomotive Superintendent Wolverhampton and Locomotive Foreman Croes Newydd". The nearest snow ploughs were based at Shrewsbury, Croes Newydd and Chester.

RIGHT: A Bala-Blaenau Festiniog mixed train passes Cwm Prysor loop in May 1950 headed by the inevitable 74XX pannier tank. *Photo: James I. C. Boyd*

Bala Jcn — Blaenau Festiniog

ABOVE: Surrounded by wild moorlands, dominated by the peaks of the Arenigs and close to Llyn Treweryn, lay the lonely mountain station of Cwm Prysor, 1,278 feet above sea level and 10½ miles from Bala, 'Halt' was added to the name as late as 1953. GWR 0-6-0PT and helpful staff pause for the photographer on 7 May 1957, standing at the south end of the single platform where a mountain track crossed the line. This merited a pair of gates, usually shut over the roadway. Note the snow fences at this altitude. During its period of operation the entrance to the loop at the north end was controlled from a ground frame 500 yards from Cwm Prysor signal box but trains, other than those carrying passengers, could only be crossed "when absolutely necessary". In the 1920 GWR Appendix to the WTTs it was stated that the signal box "would only be switched in for troop movements and on busy days — troop season only". A mile to the west of Cwm Prysor the Bala and Festiniog Railway reached its greatest engineering feat, a magnificent nine arch viaduct (still extant) over the Afon Prysor as it continued its spectacular drive down from the summit, running for most part on a ledge hacked out of the side of the mountain 300 feet above the valley.

LEFT: Busy activity in May 1957 as trains cross in the loop at Trawsfynydd, the largest intermediate station on the branch. It possessed its own water supply reservoir, substantial station buildings and signal box. The goods shed supported a lean-to locomotive shed with room for one engine. The military station and sidings, opened in 1911, lay on the west side of the overbridge seen in the distance, the two platforms and bay serving the nearby artillery ranges and training camp. There were strict instructions that "No troop train must be loaded or unloaded at the passenger station without special permission from the Divisional Superintendent". The station overlooked Trawsfynydd village which lay half a mile down the hill. Beyond, the line resumed its northerly course running through the now more gentler uplands overlooking Trawsfynydd reservoir and the Vale of Festiniog.

RIGHT: GWR 0-6-0PT 7440 enters Festiniog with a Bala bound train on 23 July 1951. The yellow brick signal box and station building were unique in design, quite distinctive from other structures on the branch. In the days of the Festiniog and Blaenau Railway, narrow gauge interchange sidings occupied the station yard. The legacy of the narrow gauge produced some very tight curves (between 5½ and 9 chains radius) on the line north of Festiniog. There were locomotive restrictions and train speeds were reduced to 15 mph in places. *Photo: R. C. Riley*

RIGHT: Continuous check rail on the F&B section of the Bala branch as GWR 0-6-0PT 7440 approaches Manod with a 'mixed' train on 23 July 1951. The narrow gauge F&BR originally opened stations at Twddyngwyn and Tan-y-manod. On conversion to standard gauge in 1883 both were closed and replaced by a new structure at Manod. Half a mile to the north lay the GWR (F&BR) locomotive shed built in 1883. It was in use until 1906 but the turntable was later retained for operating purposes as all locomotives on the branch ran chimney first unless they terminated at Trawsfynydd. The key to release the turntable lock was kept in the ground frame.
Photo: R. C. Riley

LEFT: The Shell-BP Guide to Britain merely acknowledged the fact that Blaenau Festiniog existed '3 miles north of Festiniog' and went no further, many other guides ignored it altogether or made a bare mention of the 'eyesore'. Whatever, Blaenau the 'slate capital of Snowdonia' cannot fail to interest the casual observer.

GWR 0-4-2T 5811 has just arrived at Blaenau Festiniog Central (GWR station) from Bala on 23 July 1951, and prepares to move into the headshunt to run round. It will turn at Tan-y-Manod before returning to Bala. The narrow gauge FR station lies on the other face of the platform (out of sight, left). Behind the coaching stock on the right lies the goods shed with separate standard and narrow gauge lines, seven sidings including slate trans-shipment wharves and signal box. This scene has been totally swept away and replaced by a modern ferro-concrete interchange between BR and FR opened on 22nd March 1982. Freight trains also run through the new station as a result of the 1964 connection to the former LNWR Conway Valley branch; their destination is Trawsfynydd CEGB siding or Maentwrog Road ICI Nobel siding.
Photo: R. C. Riley

Bala Jcn — Blaenau Festiniog

One of the infrequent trains carrying nuclear waste from Trawsfynydd CEGB siding runs through Maentwrog Road station on 3 October 1986 behind class 25 diesel locomotive 25201. The station, located at the point where the Dolgellau-Festiniog road crossed the railway consisted of a single platform with station building and signal box. A small yard with a cattle dock and goods shed lay beyond the road bridge to the north.

Maentwrog Road station was somewhat optimistically sited as the village it purported to serve lay some two miles distant and some 700 feet below the railway! Today the buildings have been converted to residential use and in the spring of 1986 one of the yard sidings was re-laid to facilitate the movement of explosives brought up by road from the ICI factory at Penrhyndeudraeth. *Photo: Andrew Bannister*

BALA, FESTINIOG AND BLAENAU FESTINIOG BRANCH.

Single Line worked under the Electric Train Staff Regulations. Through Electric Train Token working is in operation between Arenig and Trawsfyndd, when Cwm Prysor is switched out. The Crossing Stations are Bala Junction, Bala, Arenig, Trawsfyndd, Festiniog, Blaenau Festiniog.

Down Trains. **Week Days.**

Distance from Bala Jct. M.	C.	STATIONS.		Ruling Gradient. 1 in	Time Allowances for Ordinary Freight Trains. See page 2. Point-to Point Times.	Allow for Stop.	Allows for Start.	B	F	K	G	B	B	K	B	K	B	B	B	D	B	K	B	B	K
								Workmen's Train.	Mail.	**Goods** RR	Engine	Pass.	8.6 a.m. Glyndyfrdwy Pass.	**Goods**	Pass.	5.45 a.m. **Goods** ex Ruabon.	9.5 a.m. Wrexham Pass. **SO**	Pass.	Pass. **SO**	Empty Train. **SO**	Pass.	8.5 a.m. **Goods** ex Ruabon.	Pass.	Pass. **SO**	Ruab'n **Goods** RR SX
M.	C.				Mins.	Mins.	Mins.	a.m.	a.m.	a.m.	a.m.	a.m.	a.m.	a.m.	a.m.	a.m.	a.m.	a.m.	a.m.	a.m.	a.m.	a.m.	a.m.	p.m.	p.m.
—	—	**Bala Junction**	dep.	200 F.	....	....	1	....	**5 38**	....	**6 35**	....	*8 55*	....	9 5	9 48	*10 19*	10 53	*11 16*	....	11 35	11 51	11 58	*12 23*	*1 3*
1	55	**BALA**	arr.	L.	..	1	1	..	**5 40**	..	**6 37**	..	*8 57*	..	**9 7**	**9 52**	*10 21*	**10 55**	*11 18*	*11 25*	**11 37**	**11 54**	**12 0**	*12 25*	*1 5*
			dep.	....	....	....	....	....	▬	*5 45*	▬	**6 45**	▬	....	**9 13**	**10X51**	▬	▬	▬	—	▬	▬	**12 2**	▬	▬
1	54	**Stop Board**	,,	160 R.	..	..	..	..	..	—	....	—	Saturdays and School Holidays excepted. One class only.	..	—	—	Returns from Bala Junction at 10.50 a.m. to Wrexham.	..	..	—	..	Runs 4 minutes earlier from Bala Junction. **SO**	—	..	....
3	23	**Frongoch**	arr.	60 R.	10	1	1	....	..	—	....	6 50		....	9 18	—		....	....	—	....		12 7	....	....
			dep.					..	..	—	..	6 51		..	9 18½	**CR**		..	..	—	..		12 7½	..	..
5	0	**Tyddyn Bridge Halt**	,,	60 R.	....	....	....	....	..	—	....	6 56½		....	9 23½	—		....	....	—	....		12 13	....	
6	51	**Capel Celyn Halt**	,,	60 R.	..	..	..	..	..	—	..	7 3		..	9 29½	—		..	..	—	..		1219½	..	K
7	71	**Stop Board**	,,	66 R.	....	....	....	....	..	—	..	—		....	—	—		....	....	—	....		—	....	
8	33	**Arenig**	arr.	50 R.	22	1	1	..	..	—	....	7 8		..	9 34½	**CR**		..	..	*11 45*	..		1224½	..	**Goods**
			dep.					....	....	—	..	7 9		....	9 35	—		....	....	▬	....		12 25	....	**V**
11	12	**Cwm Prysor**	,,	55 R.	10	1	1	..	..	—	....	7 16½		..	9 42	—		..	..	..	..		1232½	..	
11	25	**Relief Sidings**	,,	L.	1	1	1	....	....	—	..	—		....	—	—		....	....	....	....		—	....	p.m.
11	65	**Stop Board**	,,	60 F.	..	..	..	..	..	*6* **P** *30*	....	—		..	—	**11P34**		..	..	..	..		—	..	..
14	42	**Bryncelynog Halt**	,,	60 F.	....	....	....	....	....	—	..	7 25		....	9 50½	—		....	....	....	....		12 41	....	....
15	60	**Llafar Halt**	,,	60 F.	..	..	..	..	..	—	..	7 28½		..	9 54	—		..	..	..	..		1244½	..	..
17	8	**Trawsfynydd**	arr.	L.	17	1	1	....	....	*6 58*	..	7 31½		....	9*57	11 52		....	....	....	....		1247½	....	
			dep.					5 45	..	▬	..	8X 5		..	10 0	12 52		..	..	..	..		12 49	..	
18	78	**Trawsfynydd Lake Halt**	,,	60 F.	..	..	..	5 49½	—	..	..	8 9½	..	....	10 4½	—	....	....	....	....	....	....	1253½	....	To convey all traffic from Tan-y-Manod.
19	75	**Maentwrog Road**	,,	60 F.	5	1	1	5 53	G	....	....	8 12	....	..	10 7	**CR**	..	..	..	..	..	..	12 56	..	
22	3	**FESTINIOG**	arr.	50 R.	7	1	1	**5 59**	Engine	..	..	**8 18**	..	....	**10 13**	**1 6**	....	....	....	....	....	....	**1 1**	....	
			dep.	....	....	....	....	**6 0**	—	..	....	**8 19**	....	..	**10 14**	**1 51**	..	..	..	..	..	..	**1 2**	..	
23	4	**Teigl Halt**	,,	60 R.	..	..	..	6 5½	a.m.	..	..	8 23½	..	....	1018½	—	....	....	....	....	....	....	1 6½	....	
24	17	**Manod**	arr.	75 R.	9	1	1	6 10	—	....	..	8 28½	....	..	1023½	—	..	..	..	..	..	..	1 11½	..	
			dep.					6**T**13	—	..	..	8**T**30	..	**9 0**	10**T**25	—	....	....	....	....	....	....	1**T** 13	....	
24	35	**Pengwern Siding**	arr.	L.	....	....	....	—	—	..	..	—	....	—	—	**2 1**	..	..	..	..	..	..	—	..	
			dep.	..	..	..	..	—	—	....	..	—	..	—	—	**2X37**	....	....	....	....	....	....	—	....	
24	65	**Tan-y-Manod S.**	,,	140 F.	2	1	1	—	**6 30**	....	..	—	....	**9CR20**	—	—	..	..	..	..	..	..	—	..	**1 45**
25	35	**BLAENAU FESTINIOG**	arr.	60 F.	2	1	..	**6 18**	**6 33**	..	..	**8 35**	..	**9X25**	**10 30**	**2 50**	....	....	....	....	....	....	**1 18**	....	**1 50**

ABOVE: In 1986, traffic over the remaining 6½ mile section of the branch received a welcome boost when trains began running from the new ICI siding at Maentwrog Road. Explosives traffic from the Penrhyndeudraeth factory was previously routed over the Cambrian Coast line but the Barmouth Bridge crisis of 1980 necessitated diversion by road to Blaenau Festiniog, for forward carriage over the Conway Valley line. This arrangement eventually proved unsatisfactory and now the transfer takes place at Maentwrog Road. With the Moelwyn range as a backcloth, class 25 diesel locomotive 25278 nears the site of Teigl Halt with an explosives train bound for Llandudno Junction Yard on 25 September 1986. *Photo: Andrew Bannister*

RIGHT: The mortal remains of Cwm Prysor in September 1986, a station bereft of trains for over twenty years. *Photo: Andrew Bannister*

Welshpool~ Llanfair

ORIGINS:	Welshpool and Llanfair Light Railway
LENGTH:	9m 5ch
OPENED:	4 April 1903 (Worked by Cambrian Railways)
CLOSED:	9 February 1931 (Passenger) 5 November 1956 (Freight)
RE-OPENED:	6 April 1963 Llanfair-Castle Caereinion
	18 July 1981 Llanfair-Welshpool (Raven Square)
	(by the W&L Light Railway Preservation Co Ltd)
RULING GRADIENT:	1 in 29
GAUGE:	2' 6"

Whereas the promoters of two of the narrow gauge lines that eventually came into the Great Western fold were interested primarily in the carriage of slate and mineral traffic, those of the third, the Welshpool and Llanfair Light Railway had the transport of agricultural requirements chiefly in mind. Incorporated in 1899 and opened for goods traffic in March 1903, the line retained its independence until acquired by the GWR in 1923, although worked and maintained by the Cambrian up to that date. It was notable for its passage through the streets and alleys of Welshpool and the fearsome climb of Golfa Bank, nearly a mile of 1 in 29/30 gradient. Happily, the latter experience can still be sampled thanks to the magnificent efforts of the Welshpool and Llanfair Light Railway Preservation Company.

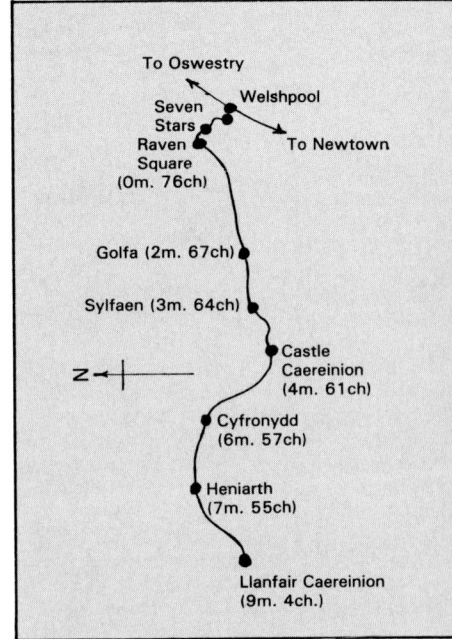

ABOVE: Welshpool and Llanfair Railway 0-6-0T *The Earl* (GWR 822) heads west through Raven Square on a fine spring day in 1956 seven months before closure by BR. During the 1950s services were confined to one daily goods train leaving Welshpool just before midday.

ABOVE: On a very misty 21 April 1955 W&L 0-6-0T *Countess* (GWR 823) returns from Llanfair with a train of empty coal wagons, easing down the hill between Cwm Lane Crossing and Raven Square. The rich woodlands of the Powys Castle estate cover the distant slopes.

LEFT: Golfa station lay close to the summit of the fearsome bank up from Welshpool and the rather spartan facilities consisted of a corrugated iron waiting shelter and 120 feet long loop. The driver of 822 closes the regulator on the approach to Cwm Lane crossing on 4 April 1956.

Welshpool — Llanfair

822's fireman climbs down to open the level crossing gates at Castle Caereinion on 4 April 1956. The signal box installed by Tyer and Co in 1907, together with signals and interlocking mechanism, originally controlled the passing loop and sidings but was never fully utilised except on Mondays (Welshpool Fair Day) and Saturdays when both engines were in steam. After 1911 the line was worked by one engine. The train, alongside the 120 feet long platform and waiting shelter, consists of eight vehicles, four coal wagons and a further two of cement, both sheeted, a van containing general goods and a brakevan. Ground frames controlled the entrances to the loop after 1931 when the signal box lever frame was removed.

WELSHPOOL and LLANFAIR BRANCH.
(NARROW GAUGE.) WEEK DAYS ONLY.

DOWN TRAINS.

Miles from Welshpool and M.P. Mileage.		STATIONS.		K Goods MO	K Goods M WS X	K Live Stock MO RR
M.	C.			a.m.	a.m.	p.m.
—	—	Welshpool Station	dep.	7 30	11 30	4 0
—	34	Welshp'l Sev'n Stars	,,	—	—	—
—	67	Standard Quarry Sg.	,,	—	CR	—
—	76	Raven Square	,,	—	CR	—
2	67	Golfa	,,	—	CR	—
3	64	Sylfaen Halt	,,	—	CR	—
4	61	Castle Caereinion	,,	—	CR	—
5	35	Dolarddyn Crossing	,,	—	—	—
6	57	Cyfronydd	,,	—	CR	—
7	55	Heniarth	,,	—	CR	—
9	4	Llanfair Caereinion	arr.	8 20	12 30	4 50

UP TRAINS.

STATIONS.		K Live Stock MO	K Goods M WS X	K Goods MO RR	
		a.m.	p.m.	p.m.	
Llanfair Caereinion	dep.	9 0	1	5 15	
Heniarth	,,	—	CR	—	
Cyfronydd	,,	—	CR	—	
Dolarddyn Crossing	,,	—	—	—	
Castle Caereinion	,,	—	CR	—	
Sylfaen Halt	,,	—	CR	—	
Golfa	,,	—	CR	—	
Raven Square	,,	—	—	—	
Standard Quarry Sg.	,,	—	CR	—	
Welslp'l Sev'n Stars	,,	—	—	—	
Welshpool Station	arr.	9 50	2	6 5	Branch worked by one engine in steam.

Machynlleth~ Aberllefeni

Constructed primarily for the carriage of slate from quarries at Corris and Aberllefeni to Machynlleth and Derwenlas on the River Dovey, the Corris Railway lasted until the summer of 1948 when serious flooding weakened the girder bridge over the Dovey near Machynlleth. Steam hauled passenger services had commenced in 1883 and an enlightened management developed and encouraged a thriving tourist traffic, the line having been acquired by the Imperial Tramways Company of Bristol in 1878. The GWR bought the railway in 1930 and withdrew the passenger services a year later.

ORIGINS:	Corris, Machynlleth and River Dovey Tramroad (Later Corris Railway)
LENGTH:	6m 41ch
OPENED:	30 April 1859 (Freight) 4 July 1883 (Passenger)
CLOSED:	1 January 1931 (Passenger) 20 August 1948 (Freight)
RULING GRADIENT:	1 in 32
GAUGE:	2′ 3″

To Quarries

To Quarries • Aberllefeni (6m. 41c)

• Garneddwen (5m. 65c)

N

Corris (5m. 0c)

Maespoeth Jct. (4m. 22ch)

Esgairgeiliog (3m. 44ch)

Llwyngwern (2m. 22c)

Lliwdy

Doldderwen Crossing
Fridd Gate (0m. 38c)

→ To Newtown

Machynlleth

To Aberystwyth

Corris Railway 0-4-2ST No.4 (GWR No.4) of Kerr Stuart 1921 vintage runs alongside the A487 Dolgellau road near Maespoeth with the thrice weekly goods consisting of two wagons of coal, an empty slate truck and brakevan. The date is August 1947.

Aberystwyth~ Devil's Bridge

ORIGIN:	Vale of Rheidol Light Railway
LENGTH:	11m 70ch
OPENED:	22 December 1902
CLOSED:	1 January 1927 (Freight)
RULING GRADIENT:	1 in 48
GAUGE:	1′ 11½″

BELOW: Swindon built pair of 2-6-2Ts for the Rheidol line, Nos.7 and 8, await Sunday duties at the old V. of R. locomotive shed at Aberystwyth on 12 August 1956, recently named *Owain Glyndwr* and *Llywelyn* respectively. Since 1968, the former standard gauge steam shed has been used to store and service the Rheidol line trains.

The spectacular twelve mile branch along the Rheidol Valley remains British Rail's last bastion of steam. Conceived to serve the prolific lead mines, it carried huge quantities of ore down to Aberystwyth either to the harbour for onward transport by sea or to the Cambrian Railways' standard gauge outlet. From the opening the management actively encouraged tourists to visit Devil's Bridge and although mineral traffic had virtually ceased prior to 1914 local goods continued until 1927, the harbour branch having closed four years earlier.

Today the seasonal holiday tourist trade represents a small but profitable part of BR activities, marketed and publicised as one of the 'Great Little Trains of Wales'.

ABOVE: The Vale of Rheidol narrow gauge terminus adjacent to the main line terminus at Aberystwyth in early British Railways days. 2-6-2T No.7, still in GWR livery, blows off impatiently on a very unseasonable September day in 1953.

BELOW: The driver of No.7 waits for the guard's signal as Saturday afternoon shoppers complete with perambulator detrain at Capel Bangor, 4½ miles out of Aberystwyth, on 19 September 1953. The passing loop still in position, shows no sign of use.

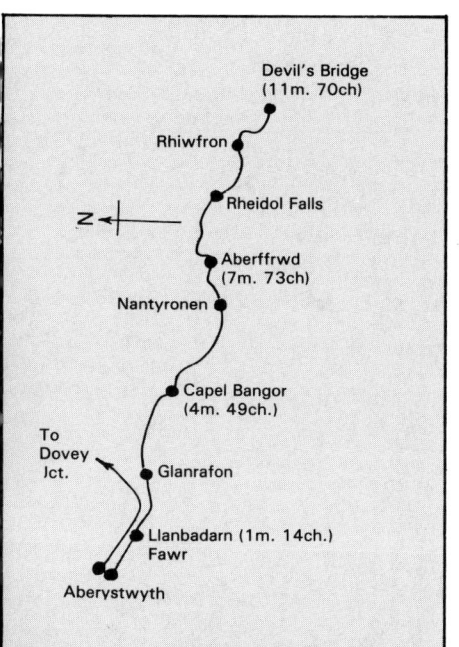

Devil's Bridge
(11m. 70ch.)

Rhiwfron

Rheidol Falls

Aberffrwd
(7m. 73ch)

Nantyronen

Capel Bangor
(4m. 49ch.)

To
Dovey
Jct.

Glanrafon

Llanbadarn (1m. 14ch.)
Fawr

Aberystwyth

Aberffrwyd and the last down train of the 1953
season as No. 7 simmers alongside the
rhododendrons. With over 4½ miles of hard climbing
still to come before reaching Devil's Bridge,
locomotive crews made the most of the water stop.